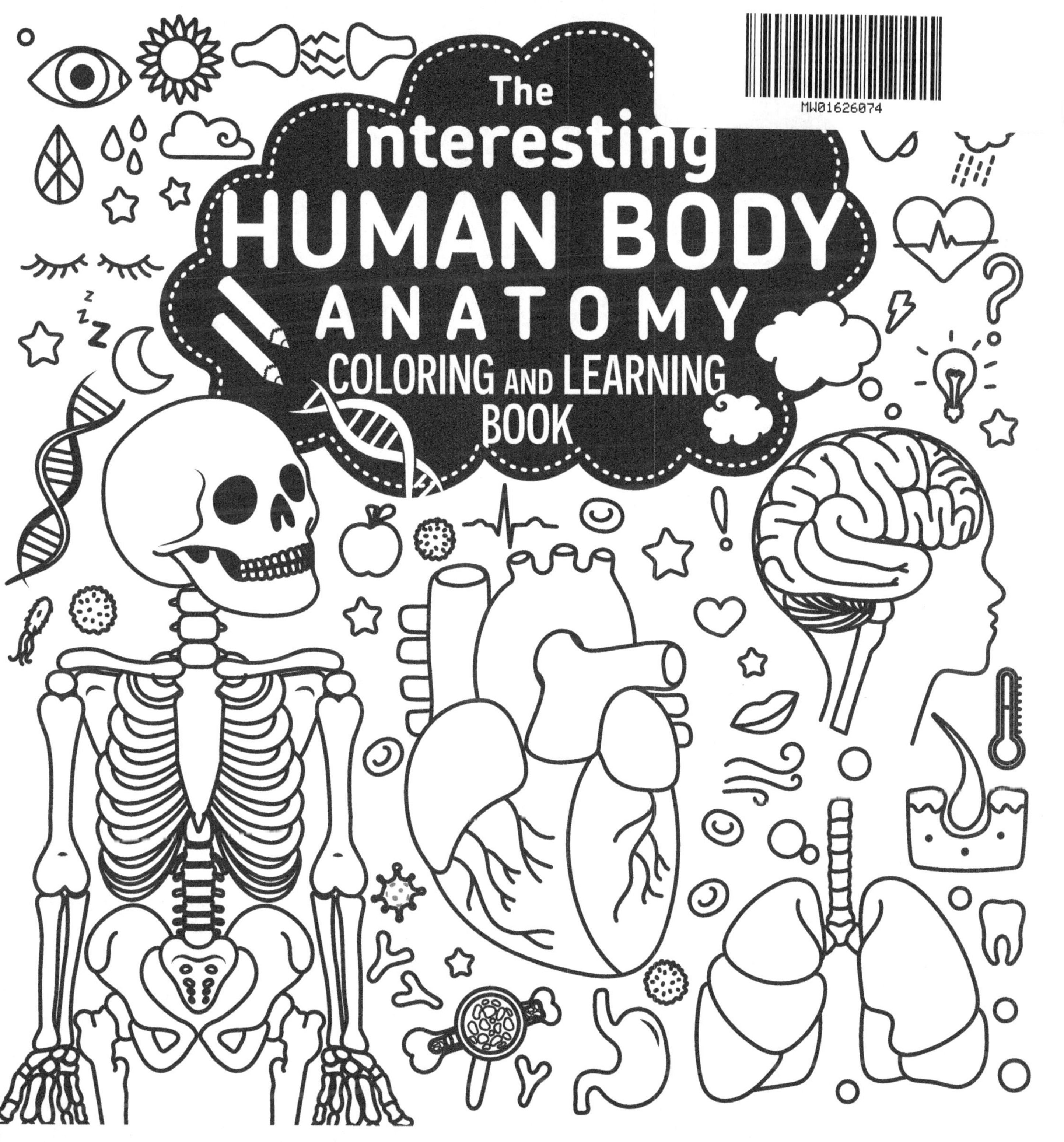
The
Interesting
HUMAN BODY
ANATOMY
COLORING AND LEARNING
BOOK
MW01626074

ISBN: 978-9934-38-303-8

This material is based on the author's medical education and years of experience creating medical illustrations. Every effort has been made to ensure the accuracy of this book's information. However, the author and publisher cannot be held responsible for any errors, omissions, or outcomes arising from its use. This book is not intended to provide medical advice or guidance and should not be used as a professional reference or substitute for expert advice. The author and publisher are not liable for any damages, losses, or consequences arising from the use of this book.

For permission requests, contact the publisher at: reinepublishing@gmail.com

First paperback edition 2025

Book design and illustrations by Gunita Reine

This Book Belongs to

Welcome

Thank you for choosing my coloring book! It's designed to make learning about the human body both enjoyable and easy.

Each coloring page is paired with a lined page on the opposite side, so you can write down your thoughts and important details. As you color, you'll find names and short descriptions of each body part. Small illustrations around the page add more fun.

To get the best results and prevent ink from bleeding through, I recommend using colored pencils. For extra protection, you can place a sheet of white paper behind the page.

Let's start learning about the human body!

Contents

Notes

Cells are the building blocks of all living things, and they have tiny parts called organelles that help them do their jobs.

CELL

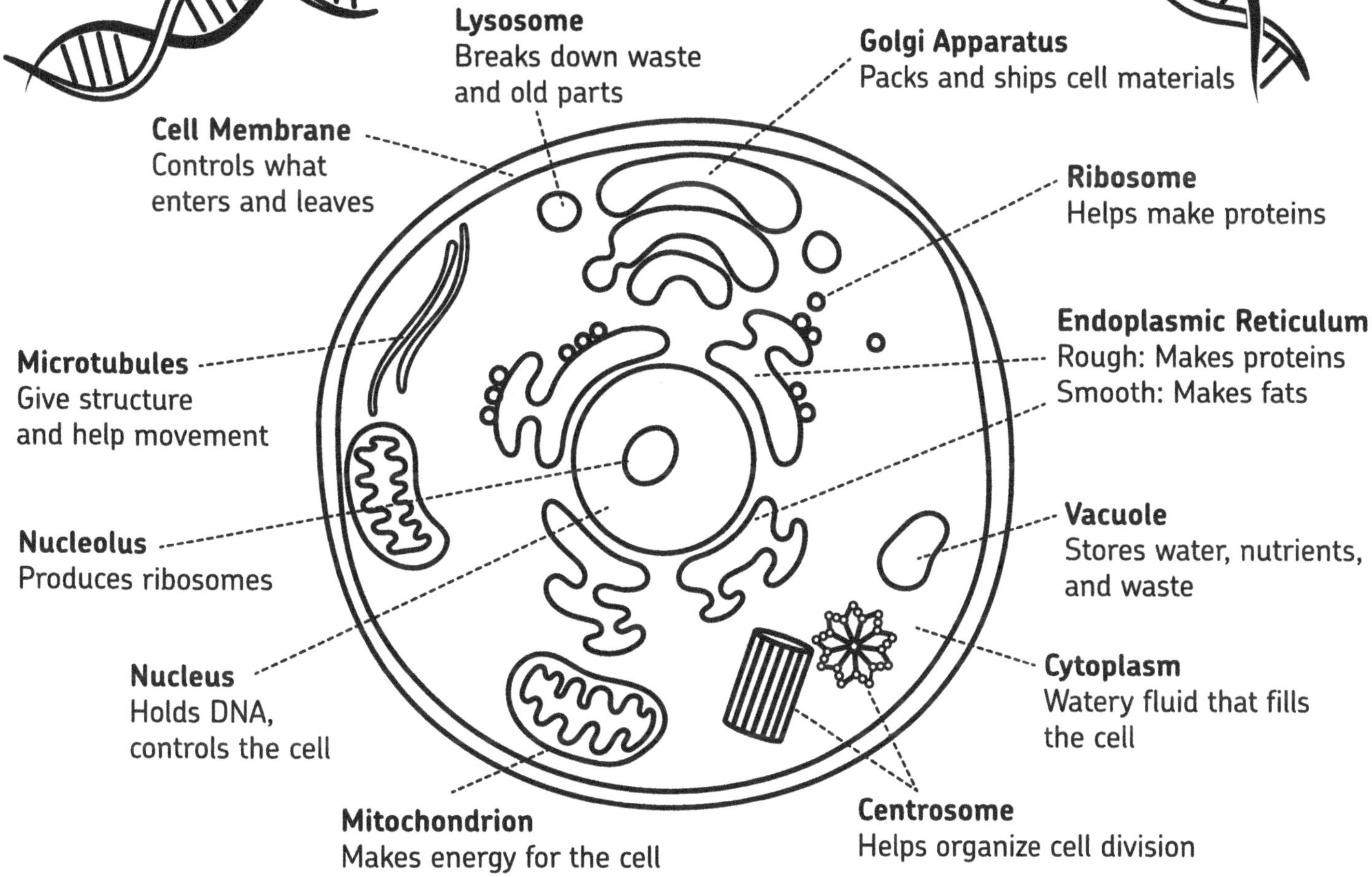

Lysosome
Breaks down waste and old parts

Golgi Apparatus
Packs and ships cell materials

Cell Membrane
Controls what enters and leaves

Ribosome
Helps make proteins

Endoplasmic Reticulum
Rough: Makes proteins
Smooth: Makes fats

Microtubules
Give structure and help movement

Nucleolus
Produces ribosomes

Vacuole
Stores water, nutrients, and waste

Nucleus
Holds DNA, controls the cell

Cytoplasm
Watery fluid that fills the cell

Mitochondrion
Makes energy for the cell

Centrosome
Helps organize cell division

SOME TYPES OF CELLS

Nerve Cell
Sends signals throughout the body

Red Blood Cell
Carries oxygen throughout the body

White Blood Cell
Fights germs and infections

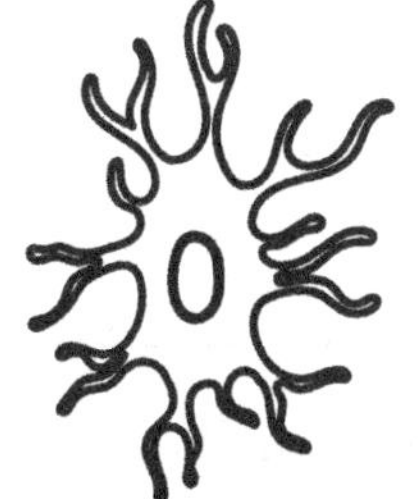

Bone Cell
Maintains and strengthens bones by forming and remodeling tissue

Muscle Cell
Enables movement by contracting and relaxing

Notes

The skeleton supports the body and enables movement with the help of muscles. Bones are made of two types of tissue: compact bone and spongy bone. Inside the bones, **red bone marrow** produces blood cells, while **yellow bone marrow** primarily stores fat. An adult human has 206 bones.

SKELETON

Inside Spongy bone
Porous and lightweight
Compact bone
Dense outer layer
that provides strength
and protection
'ellow bone
narrow
onsists mainly of fat cells
Bone Cell
Osteocyte
Skull
Maxilla
Mandible
Clavicle
Scapula
Sternum
Ribs
Humerus
Vertebrae
Ulna
Radius
Carpals
Metacarpals
Phalanges
Pelvis
Sacrum
Coccyx
Femur
Patella
Tibia
Fibula
Tarsals
Metatarsals
Phalanges
Skeleton visible on X-ray
Joint
Ca

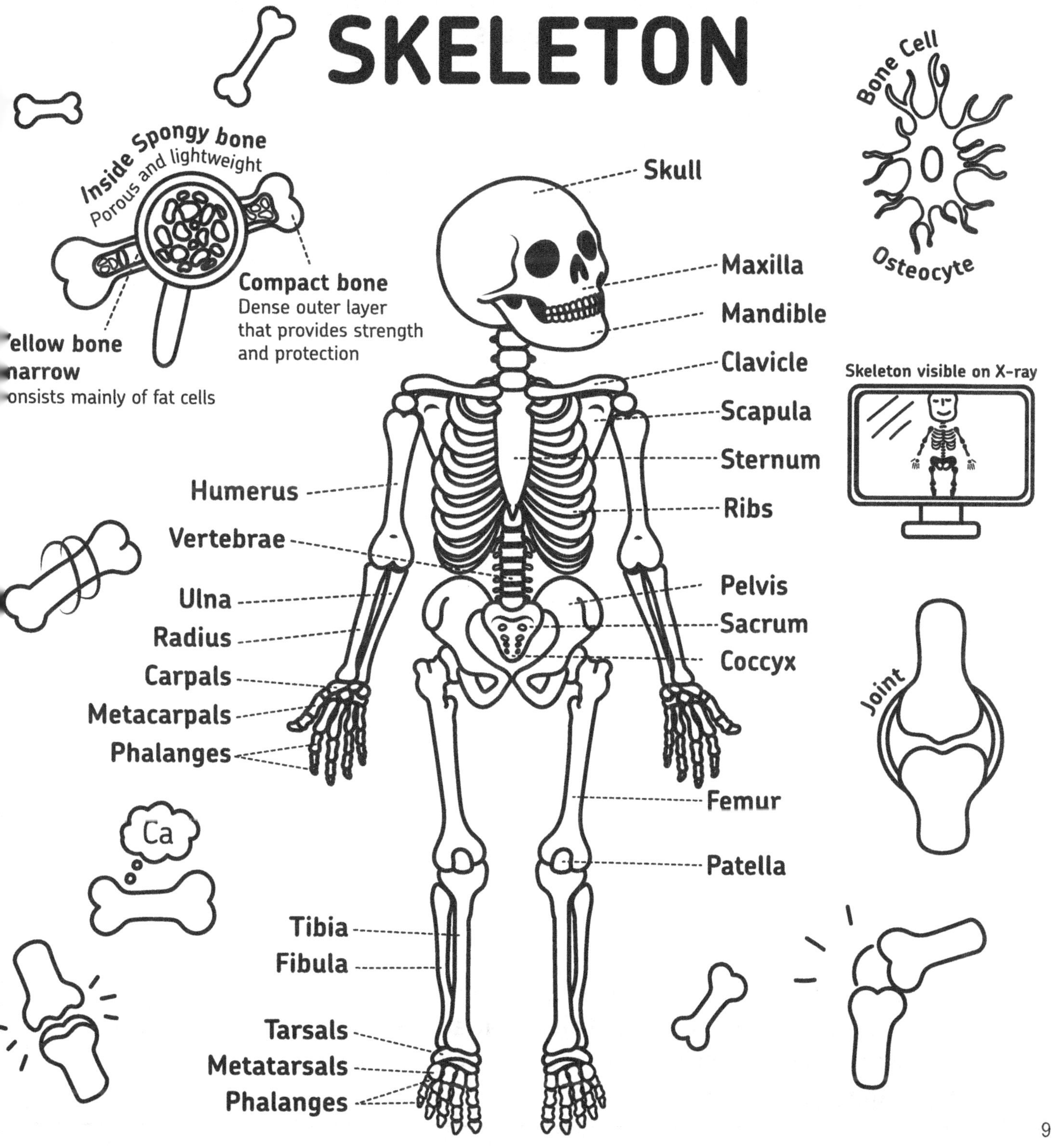

Notes

Muscles help the body move by pulling on bones and providing strength. There are three types of muscle cells: **skeletal** (attached to bones), **cardiac** (heart), and **smooth** (found in organs like the stomach). The biggest muscle in the body is the Gluteus Maximus.

MUSCLES

Frontalis
Nasalis
Masseter
Sternocleidomastoid
Pectoralis
iceps Brachii
Rectus
Abdominis
(ABS)
Sartorius
GYM
Tibialis
Orbicularis Oculi
Orbicularis Oris
Trapezius
Deltoid
Obliques
Adductors
Quadriceps
Occipitalis
6kg
Triceps Brachii
Latissimus
Dorsi
Gluteus
Maximus
Hamstring
Gastrocnemius
Achilles Tendon
5kg
Skeletal Muscle Cells
Smooth Muscle Cells
Cardiac Muscle Cells

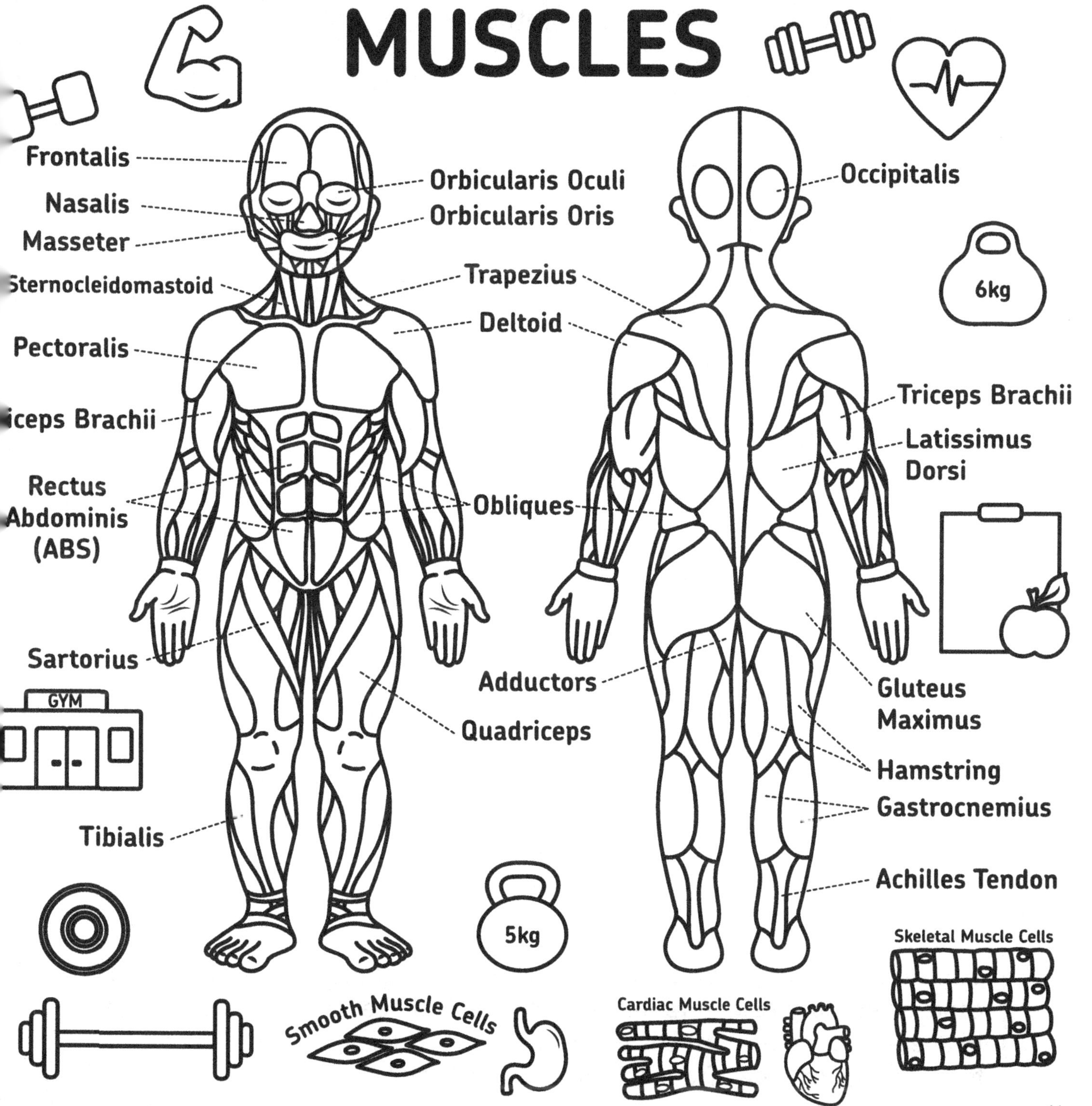

Notes

The skin is the body's largest organ. Skin covers and protects the body, and it contains **sensory receptors** that allow the body to feel sensations like touch, temperature, and pain. Hair is made of keratin, a strong protein that also forms nails, and grows from hair follicles in the skin.

SKIN AND HAIR

Hair Shaft

Sebaceous gland
Produces oil to lubricate skin and hair

Free nerve endings
Sensory receptor
Senses pain,
temperature, and itch

Muscle
Pulls hair for
"goosebumps"

Merkel Discs
Sensory receptor
Senses steady pressure
and shapes

Epidermis

Sweat Gland
Produces sweat
for cooling

Meissner's Corpuscle
Sensory receptor
Senses light touch and texture

Hair Plexus
Sensory receptor
Senses hair movement

Dermis

Pacinian Corpuscle
Sensory receptor
Detects vibration and
deep pressure

Blood Vessels

Fat

Hypodermis

Ruffini Endings
Sensory receptor
Senses skin stretch

Krause end bulb
Sensory receptor
Senses cold temperature

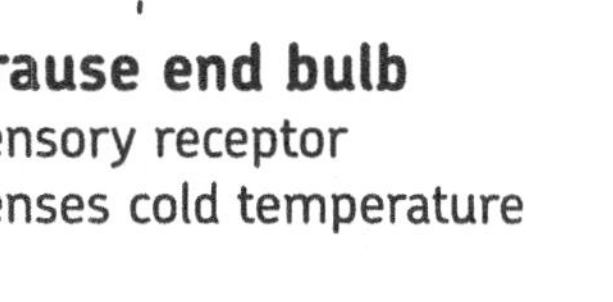

Notes

Nails protect fingers and toes from injury, enhance grip, and help humans scratch, grab, climb, dig, and more.

NAILS

Matrix
Area where new nail cells grow
Nail bed
Skin beneath the nail that provides support
Bone
Cuticle
Thin layer of skin protecting the nail root
Free Edge
Part of the nail that extends past the finger or toe
Nail
Hard surface that protects fingers and toes
Lunula
White, half-moon shape at the nail base

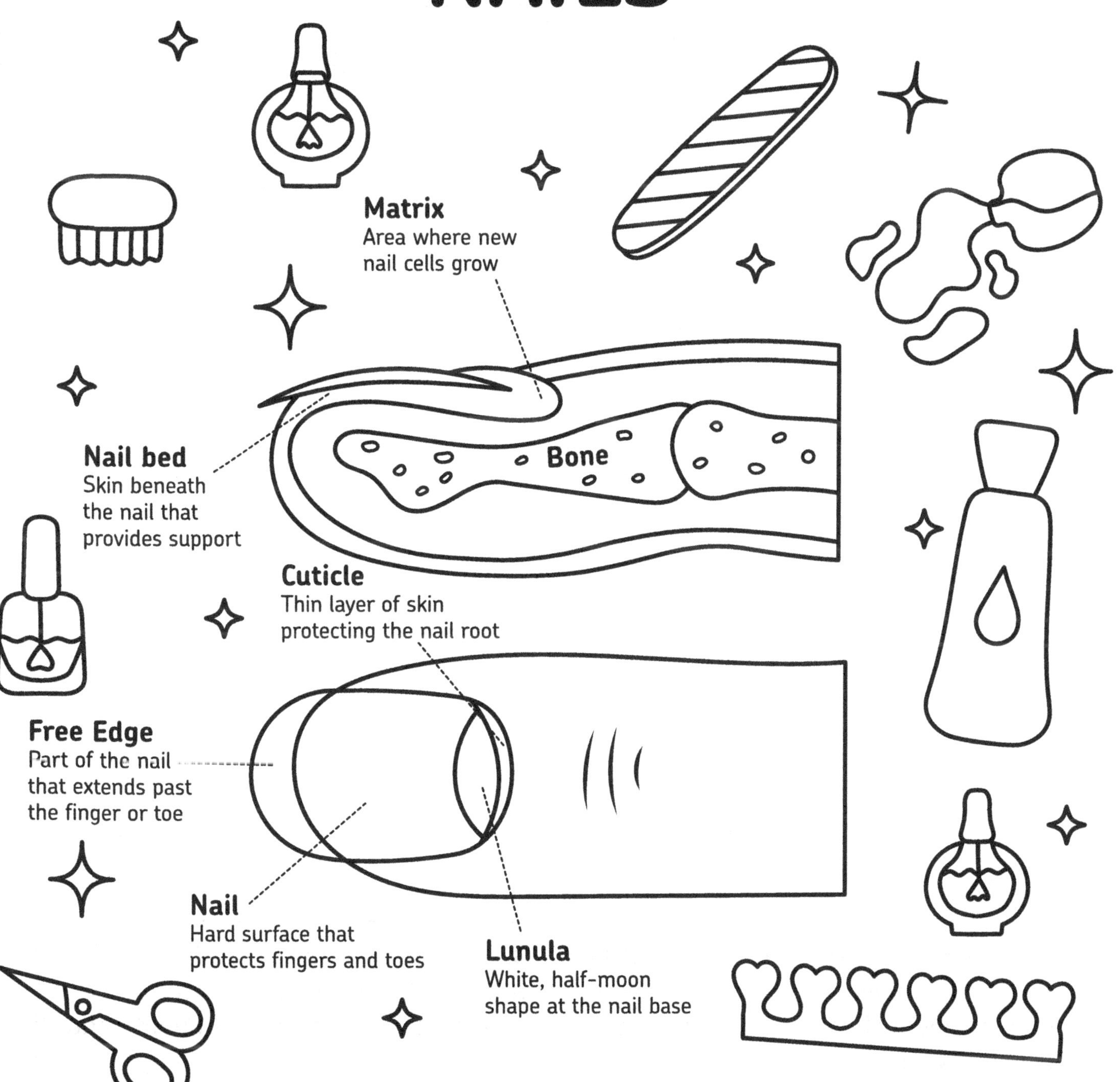

Notes

The brain, made up of billions of neurons, is the body's most complex organ. It controls memory, emotions, movement, and senses by sending signals throughout the nervous system, allowing the brain to coordinate thoughts and actions.

BRAIN

cleus
Dendrite
ll Body
Myelin Sheath
Nerve Cell (Neuron)
on
rminal
Cerebrum
Controls thinking and voluntary movements
Corpus Callosum
Connects the two sides of the brain
Hypothalamus
Regulates body temperature, hunger, thirst, and connects the nervous and endocrine systems
Pituitary Gland (Hypophysis)
The master gland that releases hormones for growth and regulates other endocrine glands
Cerebellum
Helps with balance and coordination
Brain Stem:
Pons
Medulla
Controls basic life functions like breathing and heartbeat
Thalamus
Sends sensory information, like touch and sound, to the brain
Spinal Cord
Connects the brain to the body, allowing for communication

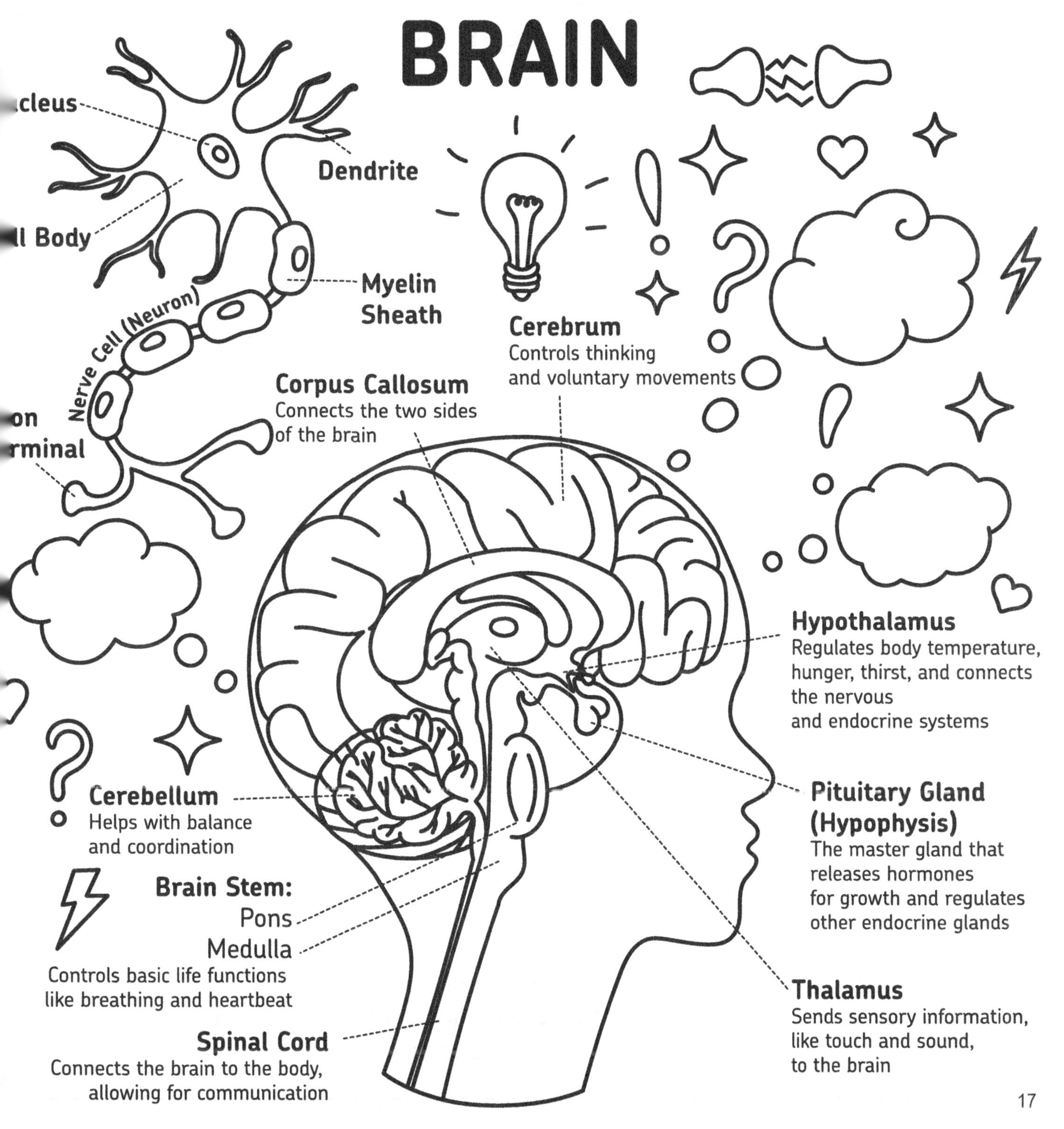

Notes

Eyes help us see and gather information about the world. Light enters the eyes and is turned into signals that travel through the optic nerve to the brain. The brain then turns these signals into the images we see.

EYE

Eyelashes
Protect eyes from dust and light
Pupil
Lets in light
Tear Duct
Drains tears from eye
Sclera
White outer layer
Iris
Colored area
Ora Serrata
Marks retina's visual edge
Muscle
Moves the eye
Macula Lutea
Helps with sharp vision
Fovea
Focuses on fine details
Cornea
Bends light into the eye
Central Retinal Vein and Artery
Supplies blood to the eye
Pupil
Controls amount of light
Optic Nerve
Sends visual signals to the brain
Iris
Colored part
Adjusts pupil size
Sclera
Protects the eyeball
Lens
Focuses light
Retina
Senses light and images
Vitreous Body
Gel-like substance

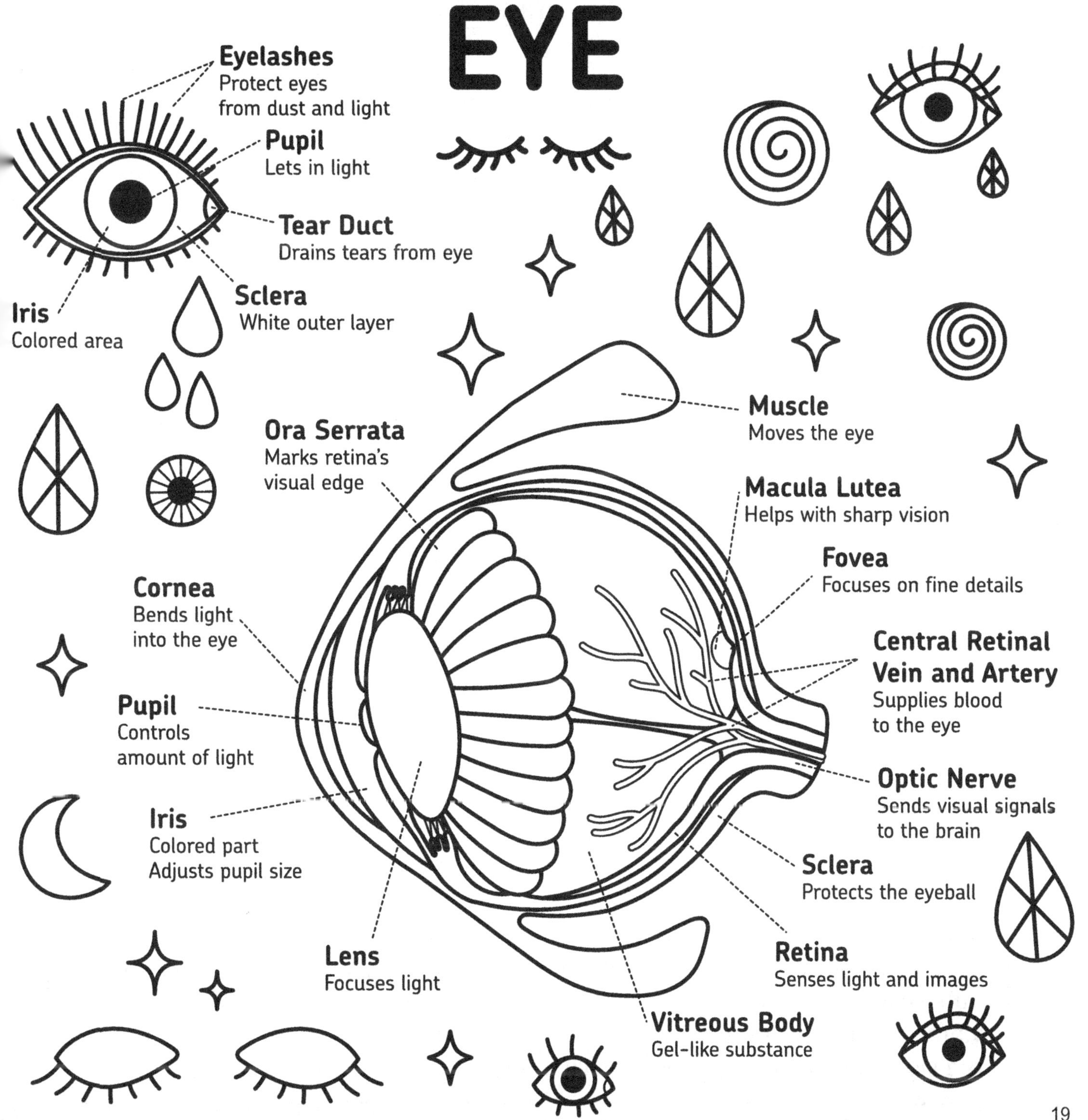

Notes

Ears help with hearing sounds and also help the body keep its balance. The outer ear collects sound waves and sends them to the eardrum, which vibrates. These vibrations pass through the middle ear to the inner ear. Finally, the signals travel to the brain, which interprets them as sound.

EAR

Bone
Tiny bones that transmit sound
Incus
Malleus
Stapes
Semicircular canals
Senses head movement and helps keep balance
Vestibular nerve
Sends balance signals to the brain
Cochlear nerve
Sends sound signals to the brain
Cochlea
Converts sound into signals
Outer Ear Canal
Tympanic cavity
Middle ear space
Eustachian tube
Balances ear pressure
Eardrum
Vibrates with sound
Lobule
Outer Ear
Middle Ear
Inner Ear

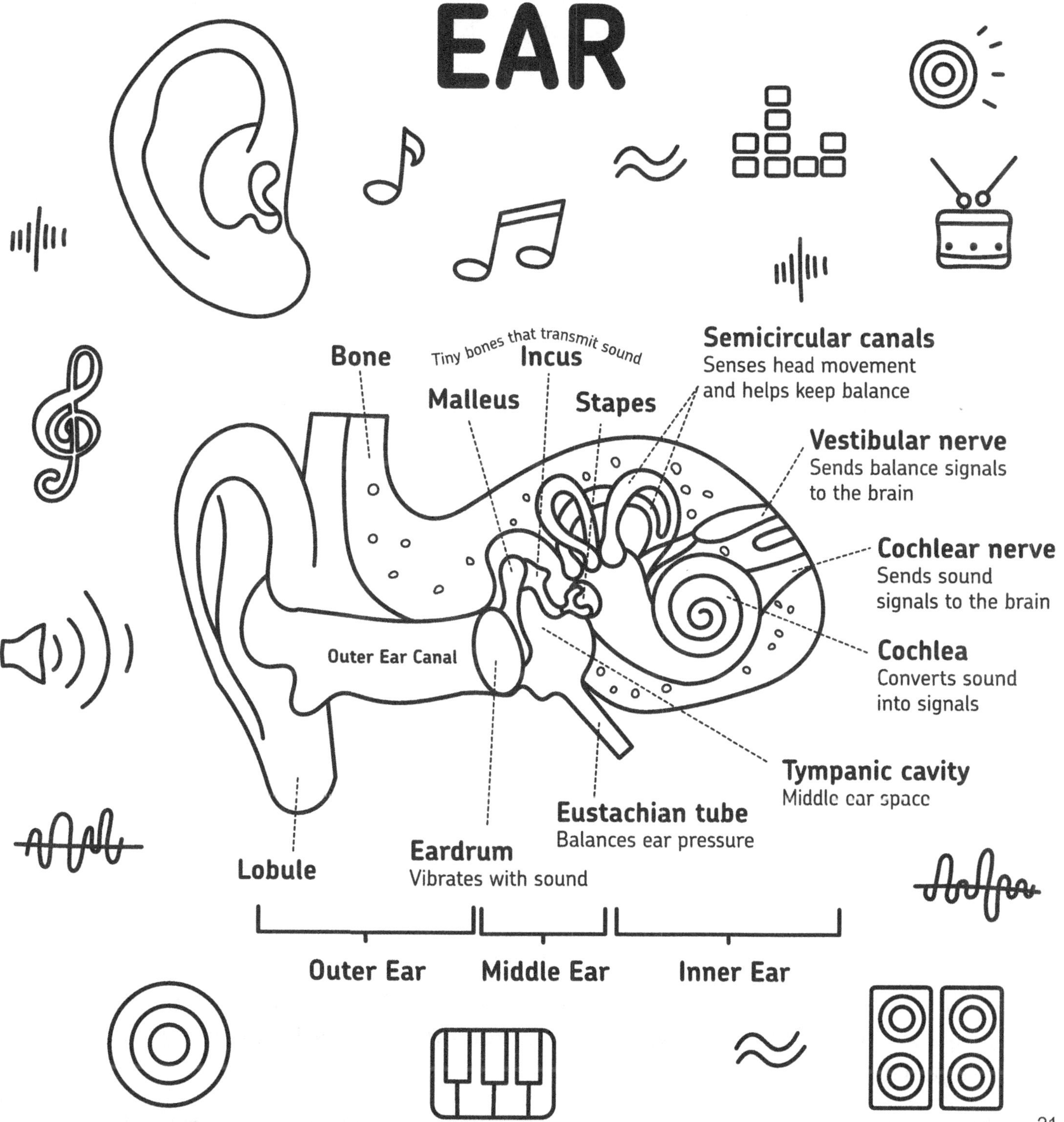

Notes

The nose is part of breathing and helps with smelling. Sinuses are empty spaces in the skull that make mucus to keep the air moist and help protect against germs.

NOSE

Frontal Sinus
Makes mucus
to keep the nose moist
Sphenoid Sinus
Deep sinus that
circulates air
and drains fluid
Conchae
Filters and humidifies air
Nasal Vestibule
Entrance to nose
O2
Teeth
Lip

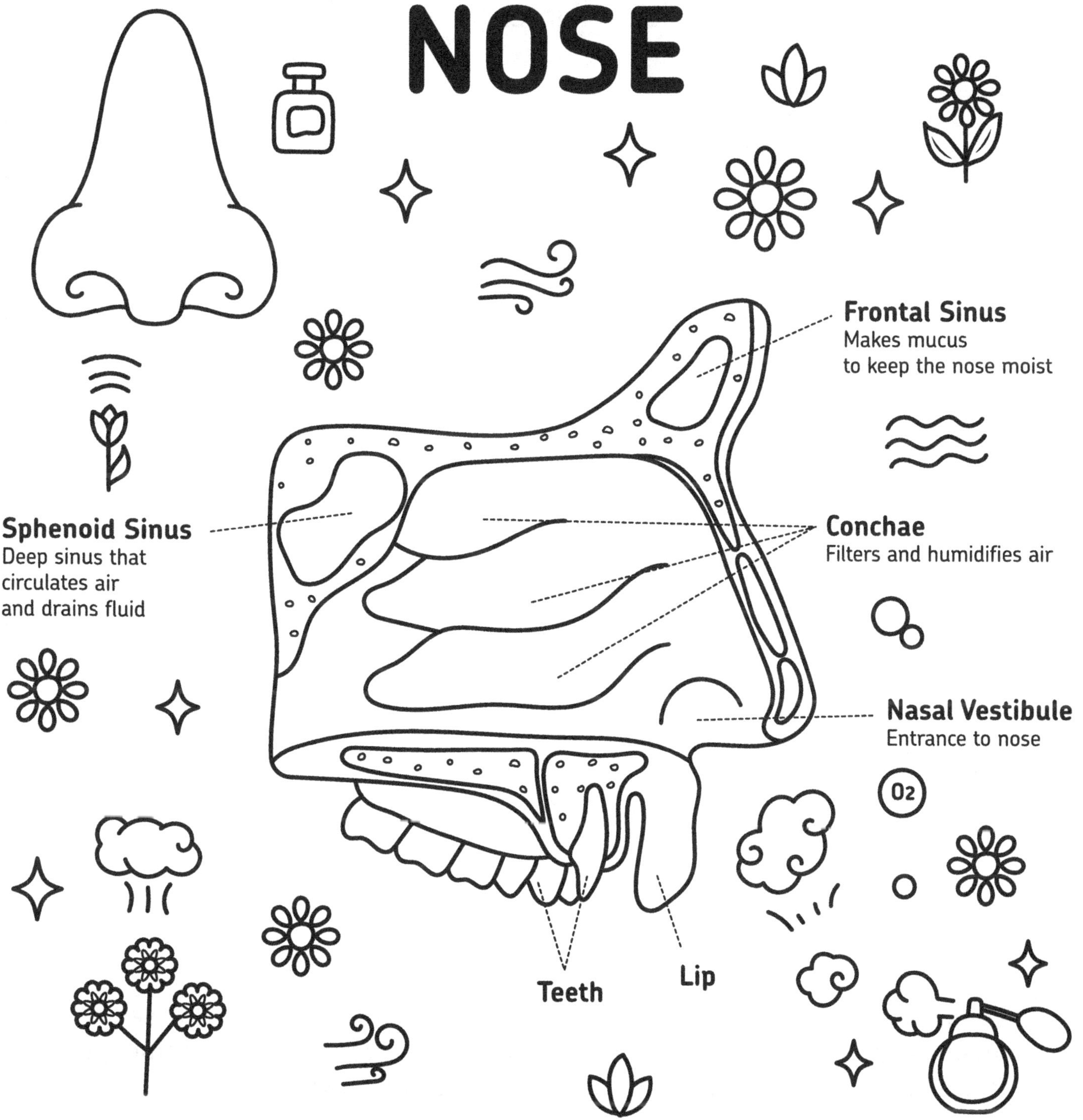

Notes

Lungs bring oxygen into the body and get rid of carbon dioxide. The nose and mouth start the process by taking in air, which then travels down the trachea to the lungs, where it reaches the alveoli for gas exchange.

LUNGS

Upper Lobe
ddle
e
wer
be
Right Lung
Left Lung
Upper Lobe
Lower Lobe
Cardiac Notch
O2
CO2
O2
Epiglottis
Prevents food entering airway
Larynx
Voice box; helps produce sound
Tracheal Cartilage
Keeps trachea open
Trachea
Main airway to lungs
Rigth Main Bronchus
Carries air to right lung
Left Main Bronchus
Carries air to left lung
Cartilage Plates
Support and keep bronchi open
Diaphragm
Muscle that helps the lungs take in and push out air
Pulmonary Venule (Oxygenated)
Returns oxygen-rich blood
Terminal Bronchiole
Leads air to alveoli
Pulmonary Capillaries
Exchange oxygen and carbon dioxide
Alveoli
Tiny sacs for gas exchange
Pulmonary Arteriole (Deoxygenated)
Carries oxygen-poor blood

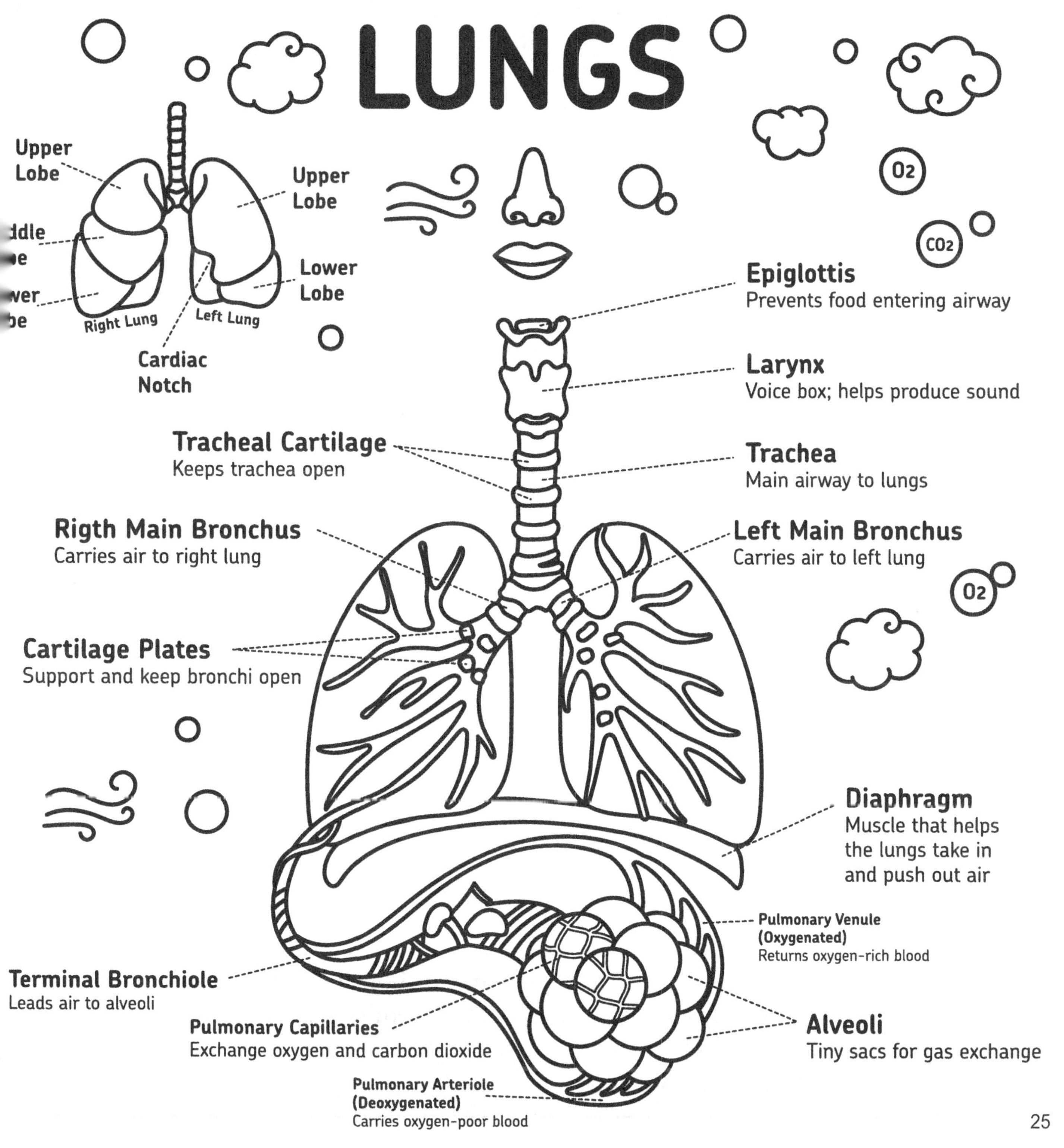

Notes

The heart is part of the circulatory system, which includes a network of blood vessels that deliver oxygen and nutrients to the entire body. The heart has four chambers: two atria (upper chambers) and two ventricles (lower chambers) that work together to pump blood.

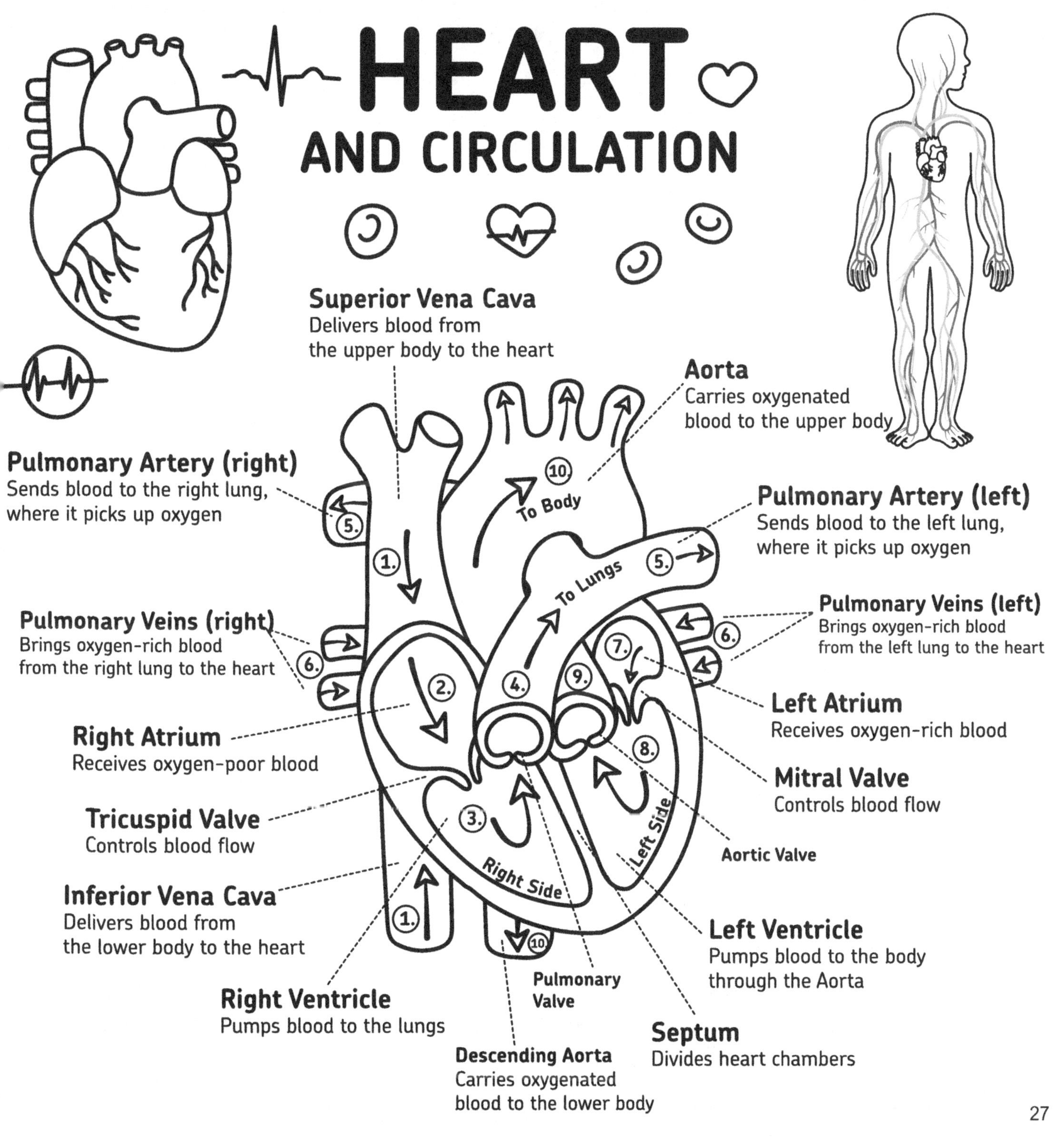
HEART
AND CIRCULATION
Superior Vena Cava
Delivers blood from the upper body to the heart
Aorta
Carries oxygenated blood to the upper body
Pulmonary Artery (right)
Sends blood to the right lung, where it picks up oxygen
To Body
Pulmonary Artery (left)
Sends blood to the left lung, where it picks up oxygen
To Lungs
Pulmonary Veins (right)
Brings oxygen-rich blood from the right lung to the heart
Pulmonary Veins (left)
Brings oxygen-rich blood from the left lung to the heart
Left Atrium
Receives oxygen-rich blood
Right Atrium
Receives oxygen-poor blood
Mitral Valve
Controls blood flow
Tricuspid Valve
Controls blood flow
Aortic Valve
Left Side
Right Side
Inferior Vena Cava
Delivers blood from the lower body to the heart
Left Ventricle
Pumps blood to the body through the Aorta
Pulmonary Valve
Right Ventricle
Pumps blood to the lungs
Septum
Divides heart chambers
Descending Aorta
Carries oxygenated blood to the lower body

Notes

The digestive system starts at the mouth, where food is chewed and broken down. It moves through organs like the stomach and intestines, turning food into energy and absorbing nutrients the body needs.

DIGESTIVE SYSTEM

Salivary Glands:
Parotid Gland
Sublingual Gland
Submandibular Gland
Produces saliva to moisten food and start breaking it down

Pharynx
Passage for food and air

Esophagus
Moves food to the stomach

Liver
Produces bile and processes nutrients

Gallbladder
Stores bile for digestion

Large Intestine (Colon)
Absorbs water and forms waste

Appendix
Small structure with uncertain function

Anus
Releases waste from the body

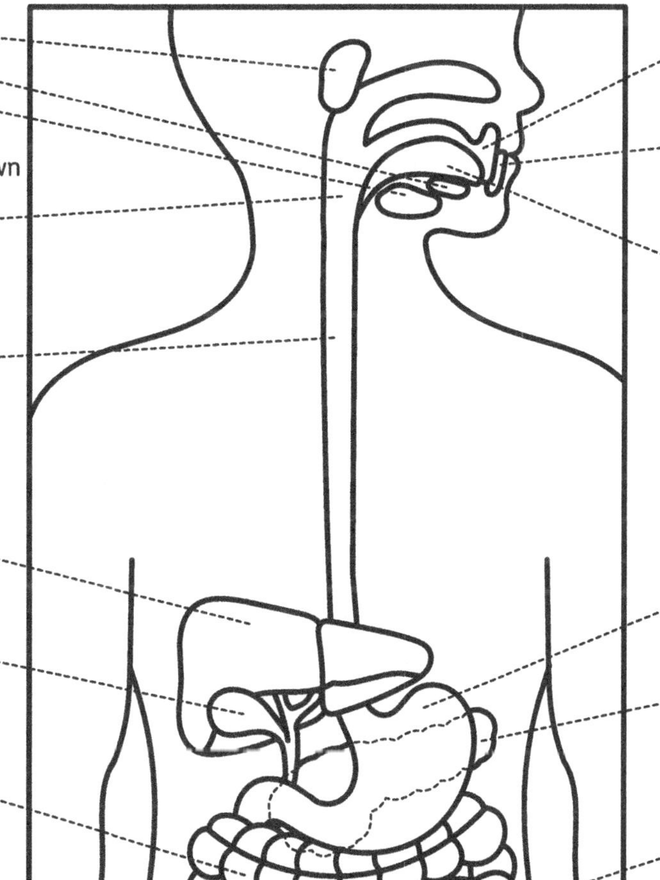

Oral cavity
Starts the digestion process

Teeth
Chews food into smaller pieces

Tongue
Helps with tasting and swallowing

Stomach
Breaks down food with acid

Pancreas
Releases enzymes for digestion

Small Intestine
Absorbs nutrients from digested food

Rectum
Stores waste before excretion

Notes

Teeth help us chew food and make it easier to swallow. They also play an important role in speech and give shape to our face.

TEETH

Enamel
Hard, outer protective layer
Dentin
Supports enamel, absorbs chewing pressure
Pulp
Contains blood vessels, nerves, and connective tissue
Cementum
Protects root and anchors tooth to bone
Periodontal Ligament
Connects tooth to bone, absorbs chewing forces
Nerve and Blood supply
Provides nutrients and sensation to the tooth
Gum (Gingiva)
Protects and supports the teeth
Bone
Anchors teeth in place
Root Canal
Pathway for nerves and blood vessels
Incisor
Canine
Premolar
Molar
Grind and break up food, with fewer roots than molars
Largest teeth for grinding
20x Baby Teeth
Tooth type and eruption time
Central Incisor (8-12 month)
Lateral Incisor (9-13 month)
Canine (16-22 month)
1st Molar (13-19 month)
2nd Molar (25-33 month)
Upper
Lower
2nd Molar (23-31 month)
1st Molar (14-18 month)
Canine (17-23 month)
Lateral Incisor (10-16 month)
Central Incisor (6-10 month)
32x Permanent Teeth
Tooth type and eruption time
Central Incisor (7-8 years)
Lateral Incisor (8-9 years)
Canine (11-12 years)
1st Premolar (10-11 years)
2nd Premolar (10-12 years)
1st Molar (6-7 years)
2nd Molar (12-13 years)
3rd Molar - Wisdom Tooth (17-21 years)
Upper
Lower
3rd Molar - Wisdom Tooth (17-21 years)
2nd Molar (11-13 years)
1st Molar (6-7 years)
2nd Premolar (11-12 years)
1st Premolar (10-11 years)
Canine (9-10 years)
Lateral Incisor (7-8 years)
Central Incisor (6-7 years)

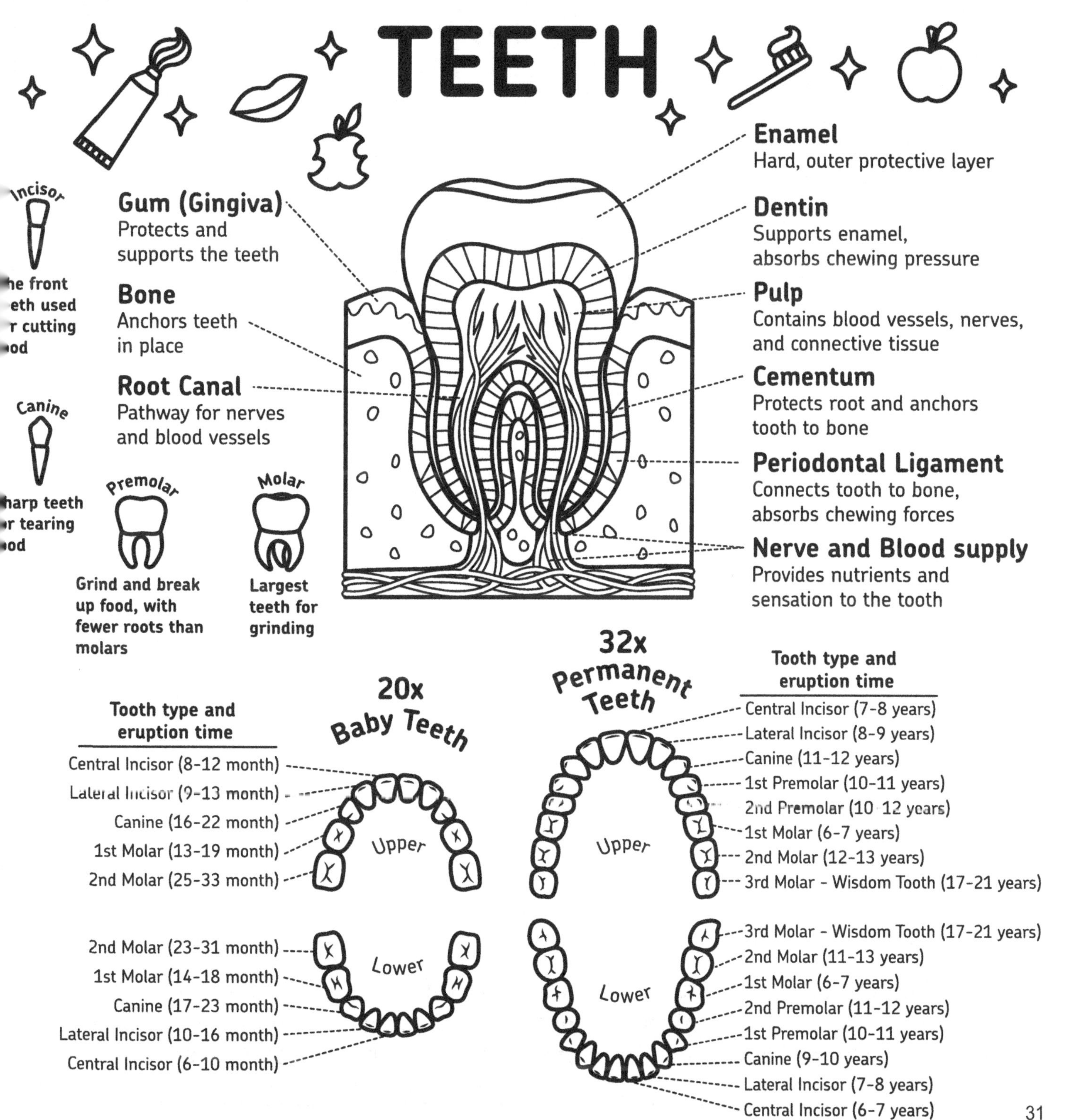

Notes

The tongue helps us taste food and move it for chewing and swallowing. It also plays an important role in speech and keeping our mouth clean. Spicy foods like chili peppers are also sensed by pain receptors on the tongue.

TONGUE

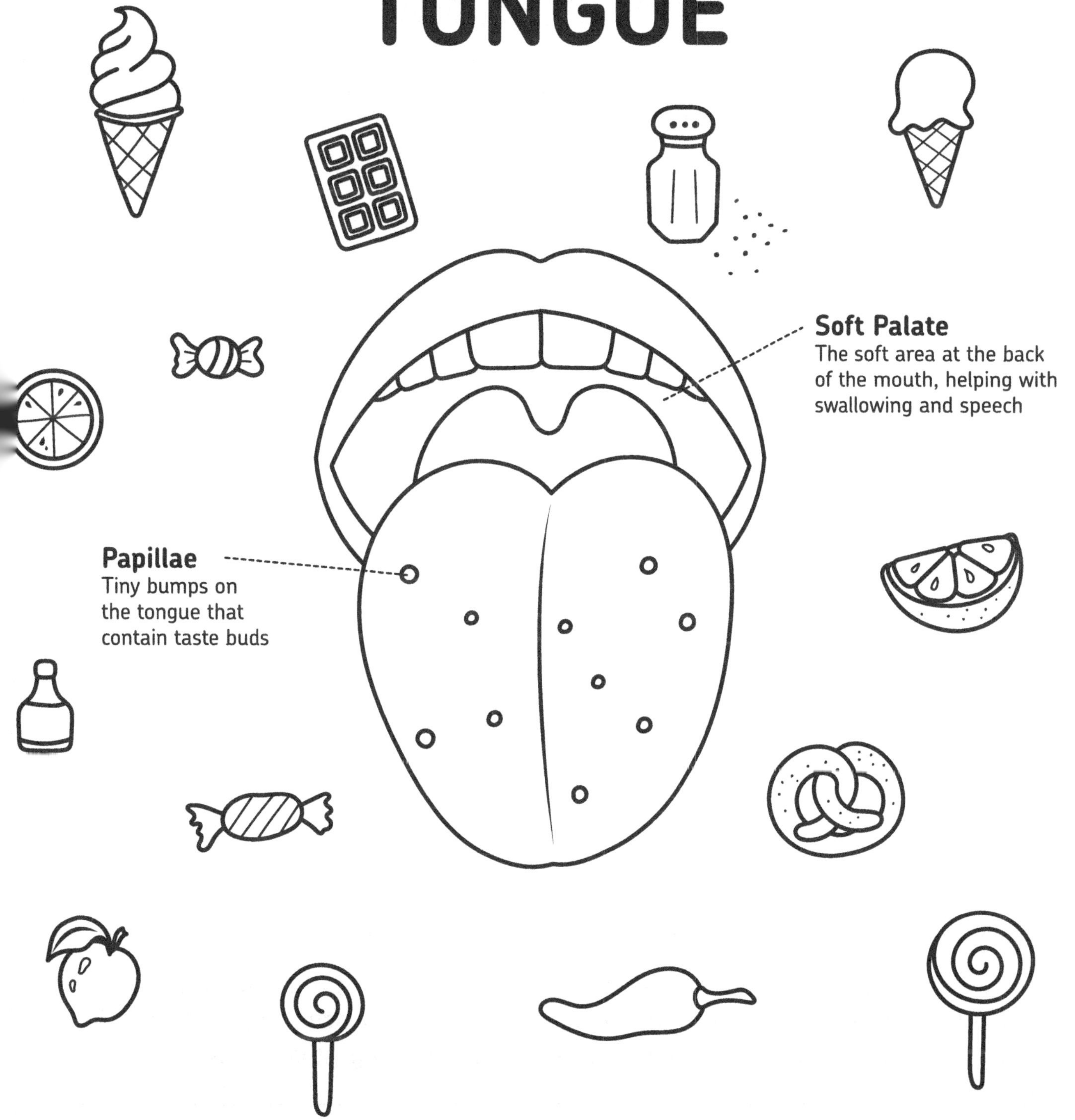

Soft Palate
The soft area at the back of the mouth, helping with swallowing and speech

Papillae
Tiny bumps on the tongue that contain taste buds

Notes

The stomach breaks down food using acid and enzymes, turning it into a liquid mixture for the intestines to digest. Its strong muscles and folds help it mix and hold food until it's ready to move along the digestive system.

STOMACH

Esophagus
Passage for food into stomach
Gastric Folds (Rugae)
Help the stomach stretch and expand while eating
Lower Esophageal Sphincter
Controls food entry into stomach
Stomach Juices
Contain acids and enzymes that break down proteins and kill harmful germss
Pyloric Sphincter
Controls food exiting to intestines
Serosa
Outer layer that protects the stomach
Fundus
Stores gas and holds food when needed
Cardia
Entry point for food from the esophagus
Body
Main part where digestion occurs
Three Muscle layers:
Longitudinal
Circular
Oblique
Mix and churn food for digestion with juices
Pylorus:
Pyloric Canal
Pyloric Antrum
Regulates food movement into the intestines
Parts of The Stomach

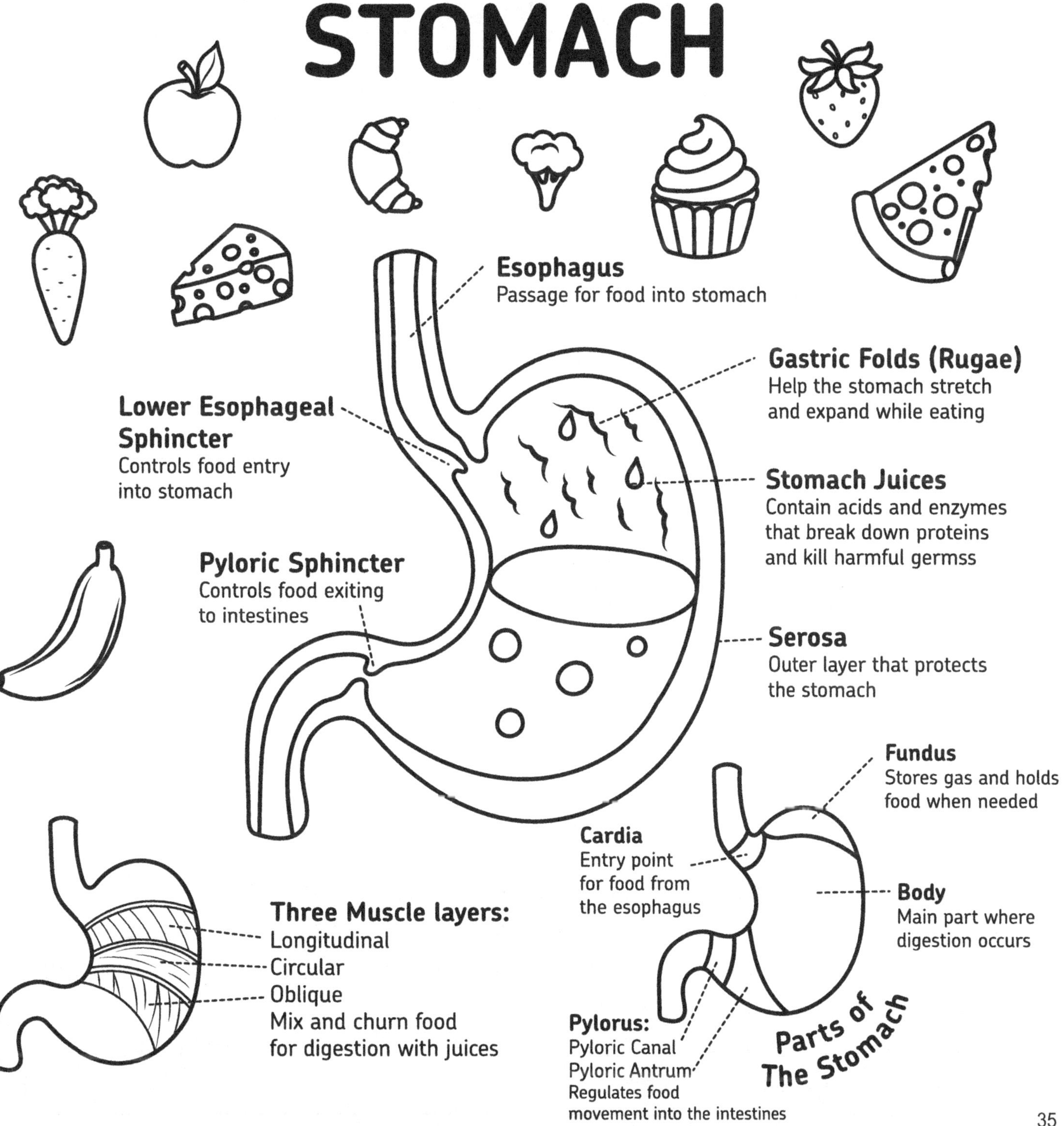

Notes

The pancreas, gallbladder, and liver work together to help with digestion. The pancreas releases enzymes and hormones, the gallbladder stores bile, and the liver processes nutrients and toxins while making bile for fat digestion.

The liver is the only organ in the human body that can grow back after part of it is removed.

PANCREAS, GALLBLADDER, AND LIVER

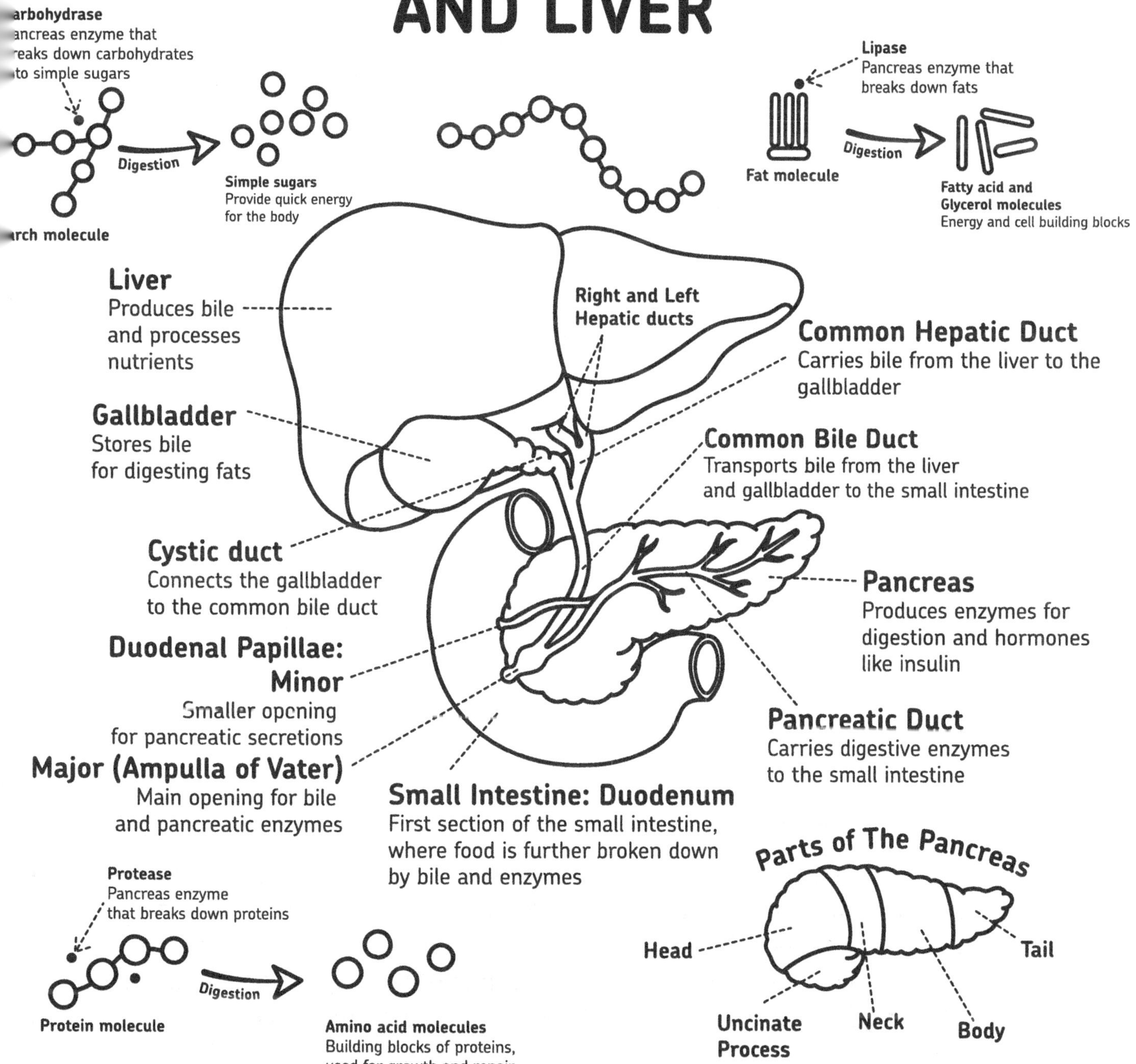

Notes

The small intestine absorbs nutrients, while the **large intestine** absorbs water and forms waste. **Intestinal microbiota**, or **gut bacteria**, live in the large intestine, where they aid digestion and support a healthy immune system. However, bad bacteria can sometimes grow due to poor diet, illness, or reduced good bacteria, causing digestive problems or infections.

INTESTINES

Ascending Colon
Absorbs water and nutrients from liquid waste

Small Intestine:

Duodenum
First section; mixes food with bile and enzymes

Jejunum
Absorbs nutrients like sugars and amino acids

Ileum
Absorbs vitamins and prepares waste for the colon

Cecum
First part of the large intestine; absorbs fluids and salts

Appendix
Small structure with unclear function

Anus
Releases waste from the body

Rectum
Stores waste before excretion

Sigmoid colon
Final holding area before waste moves to the rectum

Descending Colon
Stores waste as it becomes more solid

Transverse Colon
Moves waste and absorbs water and nutrients

GOOD BACTERIA

Help with digestion and protect against harmful germs

Lactobacillus

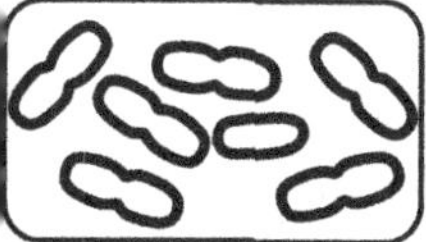

Supports digestion and fights bad bacteria

Bifidobacterium

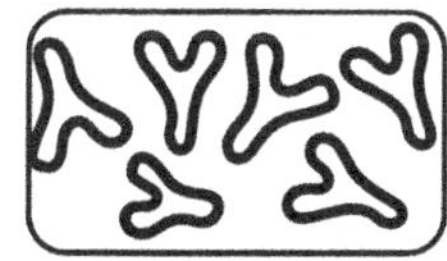

Helps digest fiber and supports immunity

Escherichia Coli

Some types aid digestion and nutrient absorption

Bacteroides

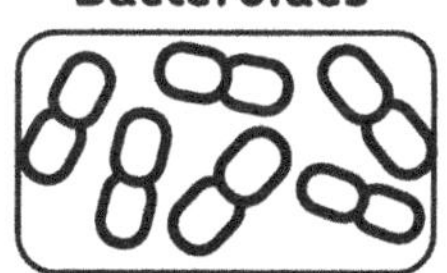

Breaks down complex carbs into energy

BAD BACTERIA

Can cause infections and upset digestion

Campylobacter

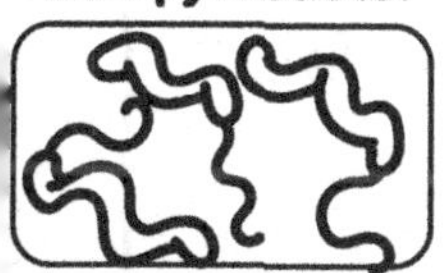

Can cause food poisoning and stomach cramps

Clostridium

Includes harmful types that cause severe diarrhea

Enterococcus

Some strains can lead to urinary or gut infections

Staphylococcus

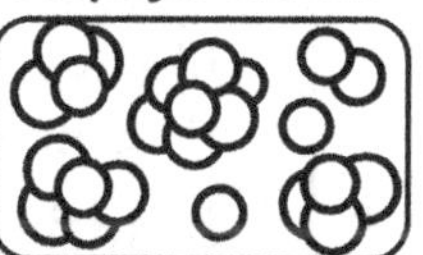

Can cause infections and upset digestion

Notes

The kidneys filter waste and extra water from the blood, creating urine. Each kidney contains millions of **nephrons**, the tiny filtering units responsible for this process. Urine travels through tubes called ureters to the **urinary bladder**, where it is stored until it leaves the body.

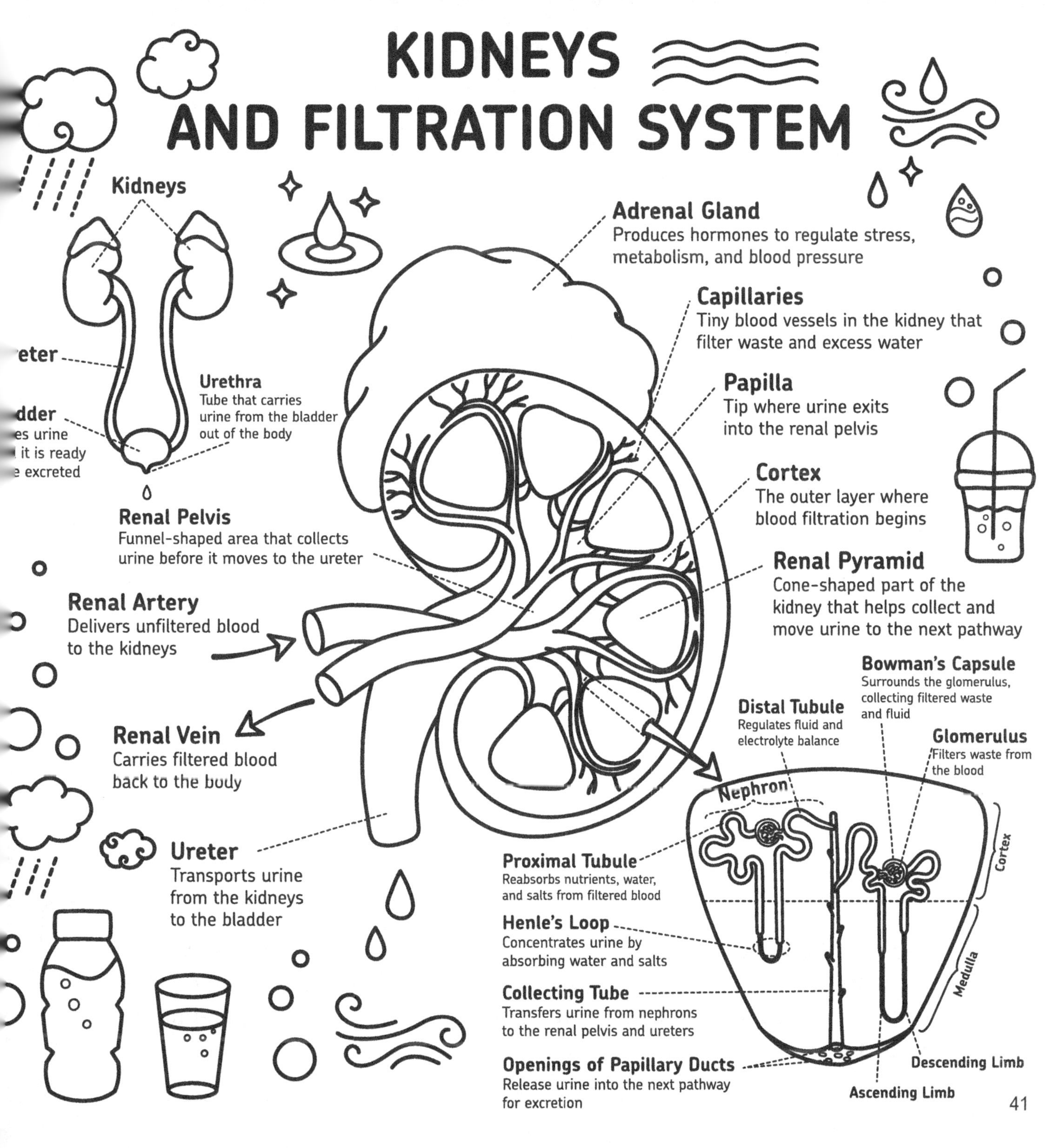
KIDNEYS
AND FILTRATION SYSTEM
Kidneys
eter
dder
es urine
it is ready
e excreted
Urethra
Tube that carries urine from the bladder out of the body
Renal Pelvis
Funnel-shaped area that collects urine before it moves to the ureter
Renal Artery
Delivers unfiltered blood to the kidneys
Renal Vein
Carries filtered blood back to the body
Ureter
Transports urine from the kidneys to the bladder
Adrenal Gland
Produces hormones to regulate stress, metabolism, and blood pressure
Capillaries
Tiny blood vessels in the kidney that filter waste and excess water
Papilla
Tip where urine exits into the renal pelvis
Cortex
The outer layer where blood filtration begins
Renal Pyramid
Cone-shaped part of the kidney that helps collect and move urine to the next pathway
Bowman's Capsule
Surrounds the glomerulus, collecting filtered waste and fluid
Distal Tubule
Regulates fluid and electrolyte balance
Glomerulus
Filters waste from the blood
Nephron
Cortex
Medulla
Proximal Tubule
Reabsorbs nutrients, water, and salts from filtered blood
Henle's Loop
Concentrates urine by absorbing water and salts
Collecting Tube
Transfers urine from nephrons to the renal pelvis and ureters
Openings of Papillary Ducts
Release urine into the next pathway for excretion
Descending Limb
Ascending Limb

Notes

The lymphatic system helps fight infections and maintain fluid balance. It circulates lymph, a fluid rich in white blood cells. The system includes the spleen, thymus, lymph nodes, bone marrow, tonsils, adenoids, and other tissues.

LYMPHATIC SYSTEM

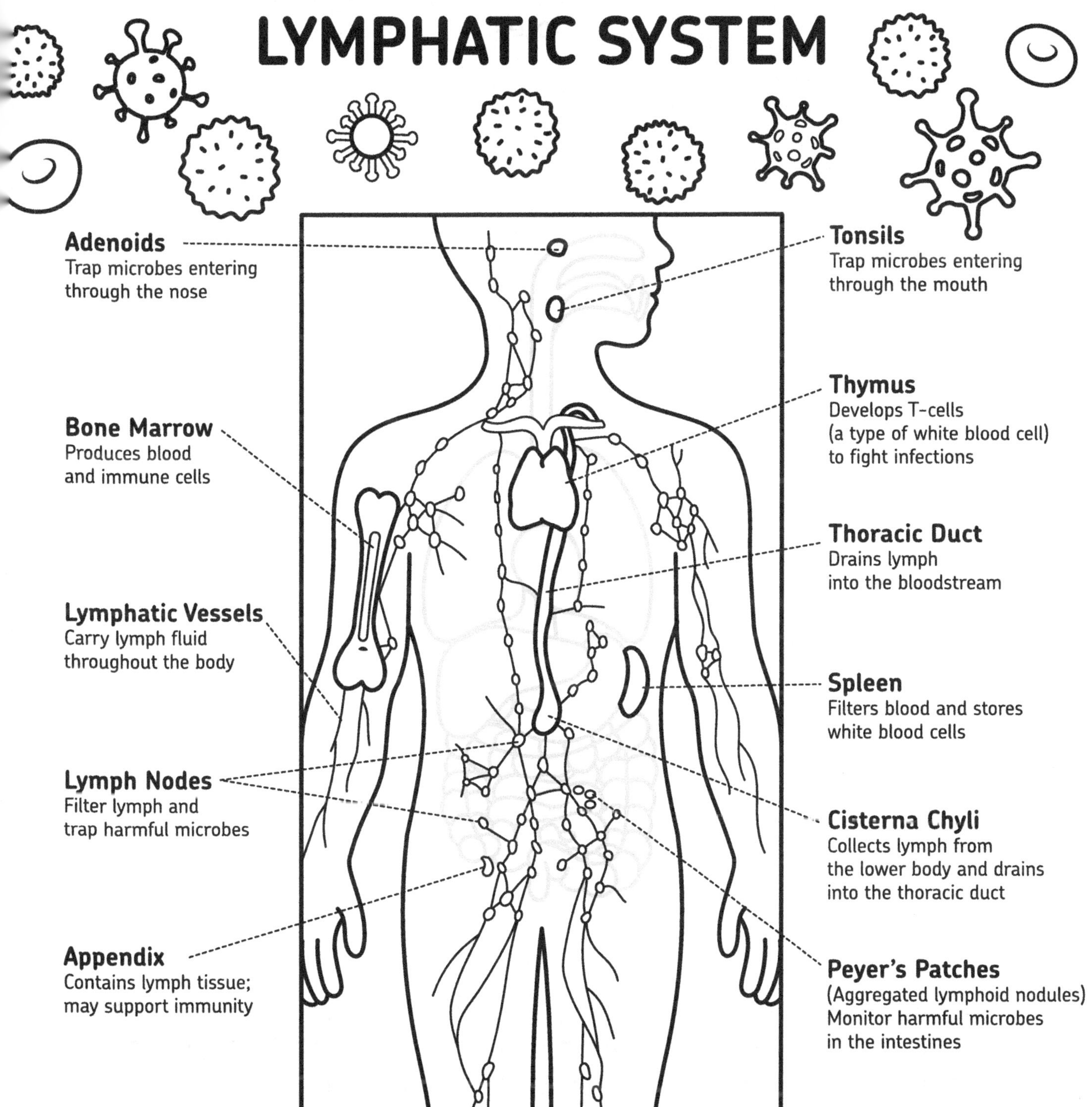

Notes

The reproductive system allows humans to have children. It includes male and female organs that create and transport reproductive cells. Hormones regulate how this system works and ensure it functions properly.

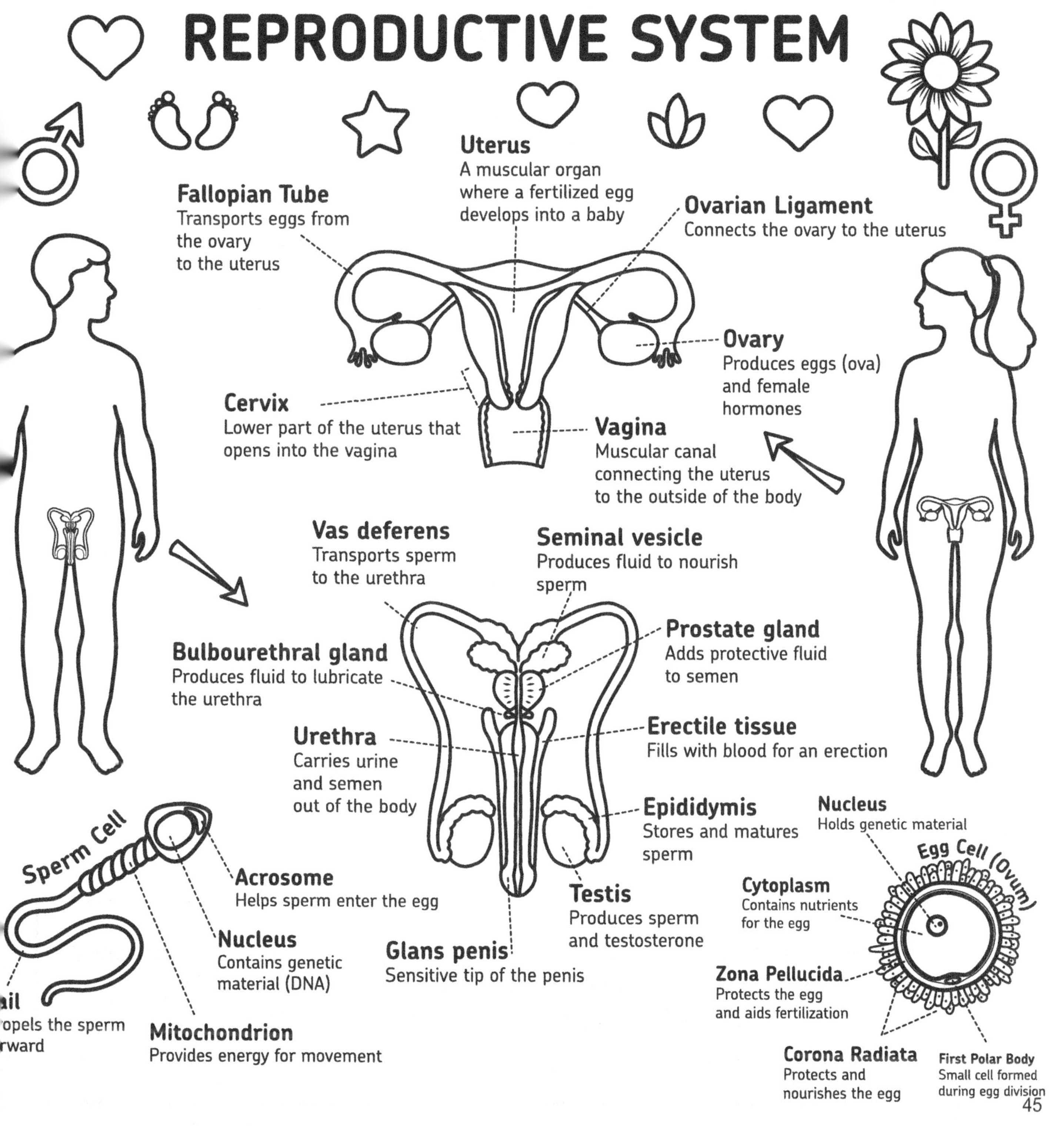
REPRODUCTIVE SYSTEM
Uterus
A muscular organ where a fertilized egg develops into a baby
Fallopian Tube
Transports eggs from the ovary to the uterus
Ovarian Ligament
Connects the ovary to the uterus
Ovary
Produces eggs (ova) and female hormones
Cervix
Lower part of the uterus that opens into the vagina
Vagina
Muscular canal connecting the uterus to the outside of the body
Vas deferens
Transports sperm to the urethra
Seminal vesicle
Produces fluid to nourish sperm
Prostate gland
Adds protective fluid to semen
Bulbourethral gland
Produces fluid to lubricate the urethra
Urethra
Carries urine and semen out of the body
Erectile tissue
Fills with blood for an erection
Epididymis
Stores and matures sperm
Testis
Produces sperm and testosterone
Glans penis
Sensitive tip of the penis
Sperm Cell
Acrosome
Helps sperm enter the egg
Nucleus
Contains genetic material (DNA)
ail
opels the sperm
rward
Mitochondrion
Provides energy for movement
Egg Cell (Ovum)
Nucleus
Holds genetic material
Cytoplasm
Contains nutrients for the egg
Zona Pellucida
Protects the egg and aids fertilization
Corona Radiata
Protects and nourishes the egg
First Polar Body
Small cell formed during egg division

Notes

The endocrine system consists of glands and organs that release hormones into the bloodstream. These hormones regulate growth, energy, sleep, appetite, blood sugar levels, stress responses, mood, and other essential processes in the body.

ENDOCRINE SYSTEM

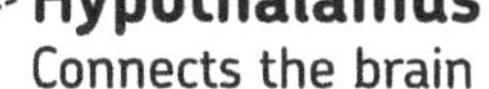

Pineal Gland
Makes melatonin
to control sleep cycles

Thyroid Gland
Regulates metabolism, mood, and body temperature with hormones like thyroxine (T4) and triiodothyronine (T3)

Parathyroid Glands
Regulate calcium levels with parathyroid hormone

Adrenal Glands
Produce hormones like cortisol to regulate stress, metabolism, and blood pressure

Testes (male)
Produce testosterone, which supports growth and reproduction

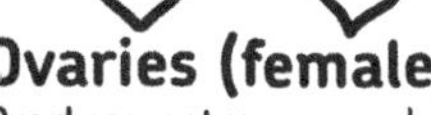

Ovaries (female)
Produce estrogen and progesterone, which support reproduction

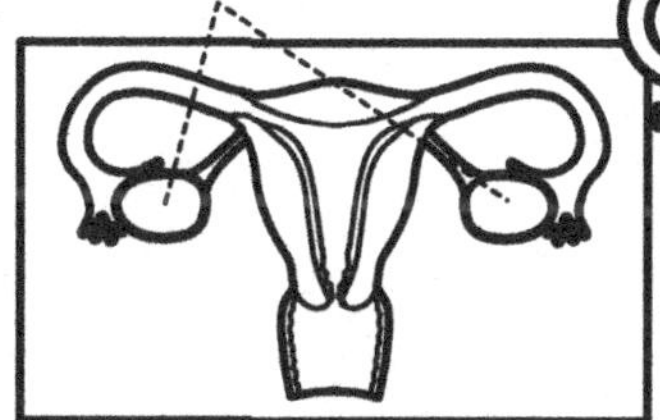

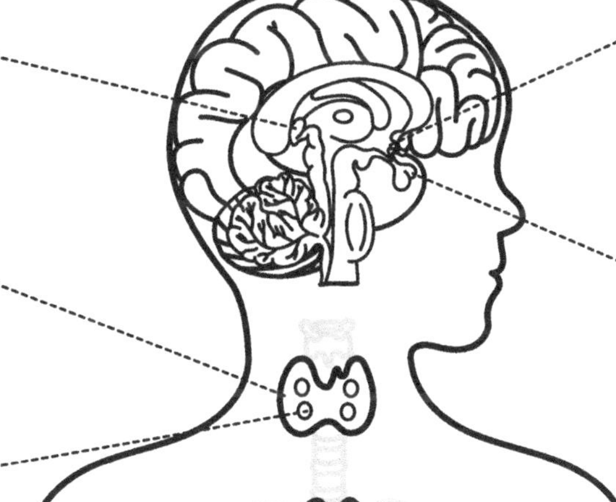

Hypothalamus
Connects the brain to the endocrine system by controlling the pituitary gland, maintaining homeostasis, and regulating hunger, thirst, and body temperature

Pituitary Gland (Hypophysis)
The master gland that produces hormones like Growth Hormone (GH), while also controlling other endocrine glands

Thymus
Produces thymosin to develop T-cells, immune cells that fight infections

Pancreas
Regulates blood sugar through insulin and glucagon production

Made in the USA
Las Vegas, NV
01 October 2025